Visiting and Grandpa

by Jeremy James

 HOUGHTON MIFFLIN   BOSTON

PHOTOGRAPHY CREDITS: Cover © Rolf Bruderer/Masterfile; Toc © CORBIS; 2 © Patrik Giardino/CORBIS; 3 © CanStock Images/Alamy; 4 © Rolf Bruderer/Masterfile; 5 © Blend Images/Alamy; 6 © CORBIS

Printed in China

ISBN-13: 978-0-547-01958-1
ISBN-10: 0-547-01958-0

4 5 6 7 8 9 0940 15 14 13 12 11 10

grandmother

We like to cook.

grandfather

We like to walk.

We like to sing.

bike

We like to ride.

checkers

We like to play.

Responding

Main Idea What is the most important idea of this book?

✏️ **Talk About It**

Text to Self Draw a picture of some older people you know. Tell about the people in your picture.

WORDS TO KNOW

I

✔ TARGET SKILL **Main Idea** Tell the main idea about a topic.

✔ TARGET STRATEGY **Summarize** Stop to tell important ideas as you read.

GENRE **Informational text** gives facts about a topic.